Is He THE ONE

BE GUIDED BY GOD IN LOVE

GAIL MARIE KING

Is He the One
Gail Marie King

Ebook ISBN: 978-1-7370914-7-9
Print ISBN: 978-1-7370914-8-6

This book is dedicated to Jesus Christ, my loving family, and the thousands of young women that God is leading to their godly mate.

If any of you lacks wisdom, you should ask God, who gives generously to all without finding fault, and it will be given to you.

– JAMES 1:5, NIV

Table of Contents

Is He
THE ONE

Preface

Is **He the One** was written for believers who are ready to stop dating and get married.

Prepare yourself to be the loving wife of a man who truly adores you. The author, Gail Marie King, shares over 50 questions that you can answer to uncover any relationship's direction, status, and health.

Learn to hear God clearly. Develop certainty regarding which relationships to keep and which to discard. Never again be taken for granted and end drifting and uncertainty.

From day one, be highly respected by anyone you date for your commitment to *both* your success. Inspire him to obey God and be a man of integrity and commitment.

Be admired by your date, family, and friends for your spiritual maturity, decisiveness, and *self-respect*.

Don't follow *world customs* that repeatedly lead to heartbreak—pivot! Stop *playing house* and get married.

Introduction

But God gives to some the gift of marriage,
and to others the gift of singleness.

- 1 CORINTHIANS 7:7, MSG

This book was written to help you become more discerning in your choice of a mate. Discover how to hear God clearly and know with certainty where a relationship is headed. Is he the one?

As we do things *God's way*, starting today, we can say goodbye to rejection, loneliness, low self-esteem, disrespect, and broken hearts.

> "I truly thank God for sharing these Christian insights with me! Before I learned God's way of mating and dating, my personal life was a mess! Now, by doing things God's way, I have joy unspeakable and self-respect. Christ has given me the freedom to love,

> but I no longer experience feelings of rejection, broken-heartedness, or loneliness. Faith takes us places that our intellect is unable to go. To God be all the glory!" – Gail Marie King

Singles the world over are searching for "The One." We have learned many mating behaviors from our parents, friends, TV, and culture. However, a little-known secret is that the Bible reveals how God leads "Mr. Right" to us.

I am sharing with you the Christian perspective and what the Word of God has to say on this subject. Read on if you genuinely wish to hear God's Word about finding "The One."

As we all know, the "dating scene" encompasses church functions, introductions, events, parties, sports, fitness groups, clubs, business networking, the Internet, and social media. It has become a billion-dollar industry. *Both Christians and non-Christians are using everything at their fingertips to find someone to love.*

Billions of dollars are invested in *finding love*, yet thousands remain lonely and are defrauded in dating scams, deceived, rejected, and broken-hearted. This book will have meaning for anyone ready to do things *God's way.*

In my own family and among my associates, I often speak with other singles about their love life. To the best of my ability, I have asked God's Holy Spirit to guide my comments then and now. My desire is to share the very best information I have learned from the Holy Spirit, the Bible, and from other seasoned men and women of God.

God has given us a way to have perfect love *all the time*. Although what God asks us to do is *simple*, it is a departure from cultural norms. We must use our faith to receive the abundant blessings God has promised believers who listen and obey.

This book was intended for believers who sincerely seek Jesus Christ and a committed relationship that leads to marriage.

This is a lengthy subject. What we will review is concise teaching that will help you understand God's will. This book will help you answer the question, "Is he the one?" You will find many revealing questions to ask yourself concerning your prospective date or marriage candidate.

Seek the Kingdom of God above all else, and live righteously, and he will give you everything you need.

– Matthew 6:33, NLT

"A tree is identified by its fruit. If a tree is good, its fruit will be good. If a tree is bad, its fruit will be bad."

– Matthew 12:33, NLT

Am I Ready for Marriage?

Spiritual and Practical Questions

As you read, take notes and meditate on the questions presented. Our ability to walk with God and obey Him releases the faith required to realize our dreams.

SPIRITUAL QUESTIONS

1) Am I willing to trust God for a spouse?
2) Have I given my life to God? Have I given my *will* to God? Have I submitted to God's authority in my life? Have I submitted to the authority and truth of God's Word in the Bible? Am I willing to do things God's way?
3) Do I truly *love* the Lord?
4) Is God first in my life, above all others?
5) Is it God's will that I marry *now*, or my will?

6) Have I asked God in prayer for a spouse?

7) If I *asked* God for a spouse, what were my *intentions*? Why do I want a spouse? Write out the reasons.

8) Am I seeking a mate to serve God as a *team* or to satisfy my own needs?

PRACTICAL QUESTIONS

9) Am I *ready* to marry now?

10) Am I financially, mentally, and emotionally ready to start a family?

11) Am I completely healed from my past relationships, affairs, or lovers? Am I over the heartache?

12) Do I find my new date attractive?

> *Yes, ask me for anything in my name,*
> *and I will do it!*
>
> – JOHN 14:14, NLT

Here's why the questions presented here are so *valuable*. First, if we do not *honor* God in our lives, how can we expect to hear and understand God's *will* concerning marriage?

Additionally, the *promises of God* are for His children. His children are those who have made Jesus the Lord of their lives. Let's be fair. Why should we seek God's blessings if we *do not want God Himself* in our lives? God has loved us even while we were sinning and following the world's ways. In return, He *deserves* our love.

> *"For God loved the world so much that he*
> *gave his one and only Son, so that everyone*

*who believes in him will not perish but
have eternal life."*

– John 3:16, NIV

When we are truly finished with rejection, deception, seduction, casual sex, and heartbreak, first, we must make Jesus the Lord of our lives.

Next, we must renew our minds with the Word of God so that we will know God's perfect will for our lives. God told us in Romans 12:2 that we must *turn away* from the world's way of doing things and *study His Word for direction*. In this way, He will tell us His perfect will.

The Word of God is living. It *speaks to* every reader or listener who uses his faith to discern the will of God.

**And be not conformed to this world: but
be ye transformed by the renewing of your
mind, that ye may prove what is that good,
and acceptable, and perfect, will of God.**

– Romans 12:2, KJB

You may be thinking, "This is far too difficult! I just want a date. It will take me forever to do all that!" Not true. Giving your life to Christ happens in a simple, heart-felt prayer.

**If you confess with your mouth that Jesus
is Lord and believe in your heart that
God raised him from the dead, you will
be saved.**

– Romans 10:9, NKJV

Commit, Submit & Dedicate Yourself

Seek First His Kingdom

Say this prayer in faith to give your life to Christ.

> "Father God, I come to you just as I am. Please cover me in the cleansing blood of Jesus and forgive all my sins. I repent and turn away from sin. I believe that Jesus Christ is the Son of God. I believe that He died for my sins and has been raised from the dead. Lord Jesus, come into my heart. Fill me with Your Holy Spirit and live your life through me. From this day forward, I belong to You. I am saved!"

If you said that prayer *sincerely* and in faith, God heard you, and you became His child. You are now a legal heir to every blessing in the Bible, which is the living Word of God. When you said that prayer *in faith* from a *sincere* heart, God gave you a new spirit capable of loving, hearing, and obeying Him.

Make sure you have a Christian Bible (the Holy Bible) and begin to read it. Also, join a good Bible-based church. As the days fly by, your mind will become renewed to God's perfect way of doing things. It will happen gradually, but I believe God's progress in our lives unfolds much faster than anticipated. Yielding your life and will to God is first and foremost. Next, we must begin to understand how much God loves us because our love relationship with God is the key to success in every other relationship.

We have compromised ourselves in unsuccessful love relationships in our past because we never knew how much God loved us. We never knew who we were in Christ, as God's children.

> **The most important relationship in our lives is our relationship with God. If we get that right, we won't have a problem with anyone else.**

Yes, there will always be people that don't like us, but that's not our business. If we bask in God's love and become able to love and keep Him first, loving and receiving love will become second nature.

How to Avoid a Broken Heart

Follow These Five Steps

Until I entered the kingdom of God, I did not realize that a broken heart could be avoided. I assumed that practically every romantic relationship ended with *someone* brokenhearted.

So we dived into new relationships headlong, spending hours talking and dating until things became more serious or someone ended it. The person who got hurt was the person who *didn't* want the relationship to end. It was just that simple.

The dating process was like rolling dice. Each person hoped he would not be the person who got dumped. Heartache was an inherent part of single life.

After I gave my life to Christ and diligently studied the Bible and Christian dating

> principles, I realized that there were godly rules that we can follow to avoid hurting anyone. We could learn to build loving, committed relationships that lead directly to marriage.

Let's quickly examine five ways anyone can avoid a broken heart.

FIVE STEPS TO AVOID A BROKEN HEART

1) **TRUST IN GOD:** Decide to trust 100% in God and obey His Word.

2) **GIVE IT TIME:** Slow down. Speed invites deception. Do not ignore the warning signs. Listen to godly advisors that you respect.

3) **HAVE GUTS:** Be courageous. Within the first 30-90 days of dating, ask your date the tough questions. Don't allow him to keep you in the dark concerning his life or concerning his long-term intentions toward you. While a man may need more time to get to know you, he usually knows day one if he is not ready to marry or he would never marry *you*.

4) **BE RESERVED:** Guard your heart. Don't allow yourself to become emotionally attached *too soon*. This is a huge mistake. Be willing to walk away if he is not seeking a committed monogamous relationship that is *headed for marriage*. If we truly want marriage, we can't *settle* for companionship; it's a waste of our time.

5) **REFRAIN FROM PREMARITAL SEX:** Reserve sex and heavy physical contact for marriage. Premarital sex blocks

divine blessings, clouds our judgment, intensifies heart-break, and promotes postponing marriage.

> **If we trust God, He is faithful. He will send us a man after His own heart who adores us and has good intentions toward us.**

Unfortunately, women's hearts are repeatedly broken because, too often, we are afraid to defend our values. As a result, we give too much too soon and to the wrong person.

MY TESTIMONY

Before I gave my life to Jesus Christ, my relationship history was awful! I didn't know what love was or how to love anyone. As a result, I could not persevere in a committed relationship.

Tragically, I did not know *anyone* who was happily married, and I came from a broken home. Without a role model for *success*, I was unable to stick with anyone.

No matter what I tried, my love relationships ended in heartbreak. I convinced myself that I was having *fun*, but I didn't have self-respect or true love at the end of the day. I thought I knew what love was, but I did not.

What society calls love and what God calls love are *worlds* apart. Few people on earth know the *true meaning* of love, and I suspect that even fewer ever experience it, even in marriage.

I now realize that I was *totally selfish* in my relationships. I could not see it at the time because, like most women, I gave much more than I should have. I disrespected myself and compromised my values, but it was all done with *ulterior motives.* I wanted men to be whatever I needed *at the moment.*

Without the Word of God, we don't know right from wrong.

I blamed the men in my past for the failure of my relationships. I no longer do that because God in His extraordinary wisdom has shown me that *I was my own problem!* I have no one to blame for my past relationship failures except myself.

Yes, the men made mistakes, too, but just as God has forgiven me my sins, I have forgiven the men. I feel goodwill toward them, and my constant prayer is that they have come to know and love God. I pray to God to bless them abundantly in their new relationships and families.

My past allows me to teach others what *not* to do. As an example, the Apostle Paul told us to constantly *warn* one another.

> **It took me decades to discover that there is nothing good *outside* of obedience to God. Abiding joy, goodness, and enduring love are in the Lord.**

After giving my life to Christ, I was able to *heal.*

I learned the true definition of love. Love is a *decision,* not a *feeling.* God is love, and because I live in God, I am love. Love *never fails.* Please read the entire chapter of 1 Corinthians, Chapter 13, which outlines God's definition of love.

Today, I've developed the integrity and self-esteem required to love my sisters and brothers without selfish motives and scorekeeping.

It's vitally important to state that Christ and Christ alone made the changes in my character. I was unable to do it on my own. However, once I began to meditate on and understand how much **God loved me**, I was able to return God's love.

> **It was imperative that I begin to see myself as God's pure and holy daughter. So I began to confess that, "I am the righteousness of God" (2 Corinthians 5:21). I confessed out loud, "(In Christ), I am pure, holy, clean, blameless, and without spot or blemish."**

Faith in Christ and the Word of God changed my entire image of myself. As a result, I cannot do what I used to do because, as stated in 2 Corinthians 5:17, I am not that person anymore.

> *Therefore if any man be in Christ, he is a new creature: old things are passed away; behold, all things are become new.*
>
> - 2 Corinthians 5:17, KJB

In loving God, it was easy to obey Him, and *I delight in His Word*. God's Word brings freedom. As King David enthusiastically said in his Psalms, "I love His laws and commands!" Through meditation on His word, His Holy Spirit revealed His perfect will for my life. I was *finally* able to *hear* and obey the Holy Spirit, and I developed a loving relationship with God *first*.

> When I meet a new man, I can enjoy his friendship without ulterior motives. I don't hurt him, nor will I allow myself to be hurt through *self- deception*.

I can hear God clearly concerning if he is "The One." As a result, I have the joy of knowing that when God presents a healthy relationship, I know because of the Word, wisdom, and voice of God. Additionally, I never feel lonely, and God has *healed my heart* from all past relationships.

> When we truly fall *in love with God*, He removes all loneliness. We become *full of Him*. We can enjoy others as we always did, but they no longer control our happiness. The Holy Spirit gives us an abiding joy that is not dependent on others or circumstances.

If it were not for the Word of God, I would have kept getting hurt and hurting others. The *drama* would have continued.

Now God has given me deep true love, peace, and loving relationships with everyone He sends into my life. Moreover, His Holy Spirit has given me the great joy of confidently expecting God's best in love.

I will never be *alone* because I have my Father God, and I *know* that He will always send me all the love I need. My heart is at peace with men, and I love them dearly.

I'm delighted about God's incredible plans for my life. Finally, the drama and madness are over, and I am not searching for love in all the *wrong* places!

God's Definition of Love

Love Freely and Unconditionally

> *Love is patient and kind. Love is not jealous or boastful or proud or rude. It does not demand its own way. It is not irritable, and it keeps no record of being wronged. It does not rejoice about injustice but rejoices whenever the truth wins out. Love never gives up, never loses faith, is always hopeful, and endures through every circumstance.*
>
> - 1 CORINTHIANS 13:4-7, NLT

Most of us have never received the kind of love that is described in 1 Corinthians 13:4-7. It is unconditional love that is not based on performance.

God deserves our love, too. In fact, He said that *obedience* is a primary indication of our *love* for Him.

If you love me, obey my commandments.

- JOHN 14:15, NLT

> **As you prepare to marry, do *not* leave God out.**

The foundation of all our relationships is our relationship with God.

If we cannot love God, we will not be able to love others. Often, selfishness can parade as love. Selfishness can abundantly give for a limited time (to receive love, sex, or commitment), but that is not *true* love.

We can go for years, giving *to get*. In these situations, we often become angry or bitter when we don't *get enough* in return, and we keep score.

To avoid painful relationships, God must be at the center of *our* lives, relationships, and affairs. When God is loved by us, He gives us the ability to love others as He loves *unconditionally*.

As we love unconditionally, we attract this same pure love, and we are no longer attracted to anyone who is *unable to love*.

Therefore, we can love others and pray for them without demanding anything in return. When we love God and have a healthy love for ourselves, we are loved deeply by others. They can enjoy our company knowing there's no resentment or secret agenda!

But first and most importantly seek
(aim at, strive after) His kingdom and
His righteousness [His way of doing and
being right—the attitude and character of
God], and all these things will be given to
you also.

– MATTHEW 6:33, AMP

God's Model for Marriage Preparation

Ruth and Boaz

Let's go to the book of Ruth. The biblical book of Ruth is *critical reading* for anyone who is trusting in God for a spouse. It is a short book, but it speaks *volumes of wisdom* concerning marriage and remarriage.

> **The book of Ruth clearly demonstrates how God *orchestrates* marriages.**

Similar to our circumstances today, Ruth lived in a culture (the time of the judges) that was saturated with disobedience, idolatry, and violence.

Yet, in Ruth, we see precisely how God incorporates faithfulness, kindness, integrity, His protection, blessings, and prosperity into divinely-appointed marriages.

In Ruth, God shows us that a path of loyalty, friendship, and a commitment to God and others allows God to bless us with a perfect mate that He approves for us.

Today, the world promotes sexual sin, lies, *deception*, and *seduction* to find a mate. This explains our horrific epidemic of sexually transmitted diseases, teen pregnancy, fraud, divorce, and heartbreak.

However, when we wake up and decide to put God first, we begin to display spiritual character and faithful obedience to God.

In turn, we receive supernaturally blessed relationships that only God could ordain.

The story of Ruth is full of revelation knowledge. Study her *character*.

Ruth 1:6-19, NLT

Then Naomi heard in Moab that the Lord had blessed his people in Judah by giving them good crops again. So Naomi and her daughters-in-law got ready to leave Moab to return to her homeland. With her two daughters-in-law she set out from the place where she had been living, and they took the road that would lead them back to Judah.

But on the way, Naomi said to her two daughters-in-law, "Go back to your mothers' homes. And may the Lord reward you for your kindness to your husbands and to me. May the Lord bless you with the security of another marriage." Then she kissed them good-bye, and they all broke down and wept. "No," they said. "We want to go with you to your people."

But Naomi replied, "Why should you go on with me? Can I still give birth to other sons who could grow up to be your husbands? No, my daughters, return to your parents' homes, for I am too old to marry again. And even if it were possible, and I were to get married tonight and bear sons, then what? Would you wait for them to grow up and refuse to marry someone else? No, of course not, my daughters! Things are far more bitter for me than for you, because the Lord himself has raised his fist against me."

And again they wept together, and Orpah kissed her mother-in-law good-bye.

But Ruth clung tightly to Naomi. "Look," Naomi said to her, "your sister-in-law has gone back to her people and to her gods. You should do the same."

But Ruth replied, "Don't ask me to leave you and turn back. Wherever you go, I will go; wherever you live, I will live. Your people will be my people, and your God will be my God. Wherever you die, I will die, and there I will be buried. May the Lord punish me severely if I allow anything but death to separate us!"

When Naomi saw that Ruth was determined to go with her, she said nothing more. So the two of them continued on their journey. When they came to Bethlehem, the entire town was excited by their arrival. "Is it really Naomi?" the women asked.

Ruth 2:1-3, NLT

Now there was a wealthy and influential man in Bethlehem named Boaz, who was a relative of Naomi's husband, Elimelech.

One day Ruth the Moabite said to Naomi, "Let me go out into the harvest fields to pick up the stalks of grain left behind by anyone who is kind enough to let me do it." Naomi replied, "All right, my daughter, go ahead."

So Ruth went out to gather grain behind the harvesters. And as it happened, she found herself working in a field that belonged to Boaz, the relative of her father-in-law, Elimelech.

Ruth goes to Boaz's field to gather food to take home to Naomi. Boaz, the family redeemer notices her loyalty to Naomi and begins to feed her, protect her, and make sure she has plenty.

Ruth 3:1-18, NLT

One day Naomi said to Ruth, "My daughter, it's time that I found a permanent home for you, so that you will be provided for. Boaz is a close relative of ours, and he's been very kind by letting you gather grain with his young women.

Tonight he will be winnowing barley at the threshing floor. Now do as I tell you—take a bath and put on perfume and dress in your nicest clothes. Then go to the threshing floor, but don't let Boaz see you until he has finished eating and drinking. Be sure to notice where he lies down; then go and uncover his feet and lie down there. He will tell you what to do."

"I will do everything you say," Ruth replied. So she went down to the threshing floor that night and followed the instructions of her mother-in-law.

After Boaz had finished eating and drinking and was in good spirits, he lay down at the far end of the pile of grain and went to sleep. Then Ruth came quietly, uncovered his feet, and lay down. Around midnight Boaz suddenly woke up and turned over. He was surprised to find a woman lying at his feet! "Who are you?" he asked. "I am your servant Ruth," she replied. "Spread the corner of your covering over me, for you are my family redeemer."

"The Lord bless you, my daughter!" Boaz exclaimed. "You are showing even more family loyalty now than you did before, for you have not gone after a younger man, whether rich or poor. Now don't worry about a thing, my daughter. I will do what is necessary, for everyone in town knows you are a virtuous woman.

But while it's true that I am one of your family redeemers, there is another man who is more closely related to you than I am. Stay here tonight, and in the morning I will talk to him. If he is willing to redeem you, very well. Let him marry you. But if he is not willing, then as surely as the Lord lives, I will redeem you myself! Now lie down here until morning."

So Ruth lay at Boaz's feet until the morning, but she got up before it was light enough for people to recognize each other. For Boaz had said, "No one must know that a woman was here at the threshing floor." Then Boaz said to her, "Bring your cloak and spread it out." He measured six scoops of barley into the cloak and placed it on her back. Then he returned to the town.

When Ruth went back to her mother-in-law, Naomi asked, "What happened, my daughter?" Ruth told Naomi everything Boaz had done for her, and she added, "He gave me these six scoops of barley and said, 'Don't go back to your mother-in-law empty-handed.'" Then Naomi said to her, "Just be patient, my daughter, until we hear what happens. The man won't rest until he has settled things today."

Ruth 4: 1-16, NLT

Boaz went to the town gate and took a seat there. Just then the family redeemer he had mentioned came by, so Boaz called out to him, "Come over here and sit down, friend. I want to talk to you." So they sat down together. Then Boaz called ten leaders from the town and asked them to sit as witnesses.

And Boaz said to the family redeemer, "You know Naomi, who came back from Moab. She is selling the land that belonged to our relative Elimelech. I thought I should speak to you about it so that you can redeem it if you wish. If you want the land, then buy it here in the presence of these witnesses. But if you don't want it, let me know right away, because I am next in line to redeem it after you."

The man replied, "All right, I'll redeem it." Then Boaz told him, "Of course, your purchase of the land from Naomi also requires that you marry Ruth, the Moabite widow. That way she can have children who will carry on her husband's name and keep the land in the family."

"Then I can't redeem it," the family redeemer replied, "because this might endanger my own estate. You redeem the land; I cannot do it." Now in those days it was the custom in Israel for anyone transferring a right of purchase to remove his sandal and hand it to the other party.

This publicly validated the transaction. So the other family redeemer drew off his sandal as he said to Boaz, "You buy the land." Then Boaz said to the elders and to the crowd standing around, "You are witnesses that today I have bought from Naomi all the property of Elimelech, Kilion, and Mahlon. And with the land I have acquired Ruth, the Moabite widow of Mahlon, to be my wife.

This way she can have a son to carry on the family name of her dead husband and to inherit the family property here in his hometown. You are all witnesses today."

Then the elders and all the people standing in the gate replied, "We are witnesses! May the Lord make this woman who is coming into your home like Rachel and Leah, from whom all the nation of Israel descended! May you prosper in Ephrathah and be famous in Bethlehem. And may the Lord give you descendants by this young woman who will be like those of our ancestor Perez, the son of Tamar and Judah."

So Boaz took Ruth into his home, and she became his wife. When he slept with her, the Lord enabled her to become pregnant, and she gave birth to a son.

Then the women of the town said to Naomi, "Praise the Lord, who has now provided a redeemer for your family! May this child be famous in Israel. May he restore your youth and care for you in your old age. For he is the son of your daughter-in-law who loves you and has been better to you than seven sons!"

Naomi took the baby and cuddled him to her breast. And she cared for him as if he were her own.

Here we clearly see that Ruth (a widow) was not looking for a husband, but God gave her a wealthy, influential spouse because of her love, loyalty, and faith. Thus, as Ruth selflessly followed God's plan for her life, she was abundantly blessed.

Both King David and Jesus were descendants of Boaz and Ruth. Therefore, we know that God chose Boaz for Ruth in His divine plan for their lives.

Ruth would not have met Boaz if she had not followed God through her love and loyalty to Naomi. As we "do right" in all areas of our lives, it sets us up to receive God's best.

Although I have heard Christians testify that they met their spouses in unlikely settings, we do *not* have to *rely on* the Internet or secular dating venues to connect with our future spouses. Instead, God can use our daily environment and faithful obedience to bring us into the presence of *kings*!

> Do you want to **search** for a mate, or do you want God to simply put His choice in your everyday path? God is faithful. God will faithfully **show you** your mate as you serve Him!

Love toward God, faith, and obedience to God's will are the keys to receiving God's *best*.

I highly recommend the reading of Genesis Chapter 24 (the love story of Isaac and Rebekah) for another powerful example of how God uses love, faith, prayer, and obedience to divinely orchestrate our marriages.

Is This Relationship Positioned to Succeed or Fail?

Evaluate the Pros and Cons of a Relationship

Ask yourself the following spiritual questions and take notes.

1. Is he saved? Is he a Christian? Has he given his life to Christ?
2. Does he have a relationship with God?
3. Is God first in his life?
4. Does he love God enough to obey Him? Is he in submission to the Word of God?
5. Does he belong to a church and fellowship with other Christians?
6. Has he discovered God's vision and will for his life? This is evidenced in his career and contributions to the lives of others.

7. Does he encourage you to obey God in terms of purity, or does he encourage you to disobey by engaging in heavy foreplay and premarital sex? Is he helping you get closer to God or move further away? Do you find yourself disobeying God to do things *his* way?

8. Do you have the *spiritual covering* of someone in your life who loves God and can be trusted to give you godly advice? If so, do they think your current date is "The One?"

9. Do you believe that your date is God's *best* for you?

10. Does he respect your walk with God?

Obtain answers to these practical questions.

1. Is he over his past relationships and lovers?

2. Is he financially secure enough to start a new family? Is he prone to spending or saving? Does he have unpaid debts and fines? If so, exactly how much? If you are both contemplating marriage, you deserve to know this information.

3. Is he single? Note: If he is *separated* from a former spouse, he is *not* single.

4. Do you respect him enough to listen to him and value his advice?

5. Does he believe household chores should be completed by you or divided?

6. Does he respect you?

7. Does he lie? Have you caught him exaggerating and telling half-truths?

8. Does he have a loving, healthy relationship with his parents, siblings, co-workers, and children?

9. Does he deliberately try to manipulate or hurt you through jealousy? For example, does he often tell you

information about other admirers to appear more desirable and to get more attention?

10. Does he have a wandering eye? Do you sense he may not be a faithful person? Is he a public flirt? Does he disappear or *come up missing* often?

11. Does he have good credit? Does he pay his bills on time? Does he live within his means? Is he 100% self-supportive?

12. If he has children, does he financially support them? Is he involved in their lives, and does he keep in touch with them? (Do not allow any man to use the children's mother as his *excuse* for not financially supporting his children.)

13. Does he remember birthdays and other days that are significant to loved ones?

14. Can you both love and spend time with extended families? Have you met them?

15. Is he seeking marriage and commitment *now*? Can you discuss this openly and candidly with him?

16. If he was previously married and children are involved, does he respect and get along with his ex?

17. Is he willing to talk candidly about both your sexual expectations? Is there any known sexual dysfunction?

18. Is he sanitary, clean, neat, and organized? Is this important to you?

19. How does he spend his leisure time?

20. Is he a drinker? How often does he drink?

21. Has he ever hit anyone or been involved in domestic violence?

22. If he has a criminal record, has he disclosed the details to you?

23. What is the condition of his health? Is he on medication? How long will he need to take it? Does it have unpleasant side effects such as impotence?

24. Are you both in agreement with your health habits and lifestyle?

25. What are his beliefs concerning monogamy and faithfulness?

26. Where would he like to be in 5, 15, and 30 years?

27. Does he trust you? Do you trust him? Do you feel secure with him?

28. Does he listen to you? Does he respect your opinion? Do you enjoy listening to him? If not, why not?

29. Does he like to go out alone, pursue his own interests, and spend time alone? Note: This can be healthy or unhealthy depending on his activities.

30. How many children does he have?

31. How many children does he want?

32. Does he have children that have become estranged? Does he have a plan to mend or improve his relationship with his children?

33. Is he willing to be mutually tested for sexually transmitted diseases *before* marriage?

34. Is he willing to submit to a background check? Is he ready to amicably discuss intentions concerning family property that you both may hold for heirs and children of previous marriages?

35. Does he have the capacity to forgive often and easily?

36. Can he maintain a respectful attitude when he is disappointed?

37. Does he want you to lose weight, change your diet, become organized, or change in some other way?

Note: You should be in agreement concerning improvements you want to make in your life, but he should not harass or belittle you.

This list is not exhaustive, but it will help you think clearly about the serious decision to marry.

Yes, we depend entirely *on God*, and we can trust Him. However, the Word of God tells us plainly to guard our hearts and to be careful.

> *Guard your heart above all else, for it determines the course of your life.*
>
> – Proverbs 4:23, NLT

> *"Behold, I send you out as sheep in the midst of wolves. Therefore be wise as serpents and harmless as doves."*
>
> – Matthew 10:16, NKJV

No One Is Perfect...

Value Character, Responsibility, Commitment

> *Be kind and helpful to one another, tender-hearted [compassionate, understanding], forgiving one another [readily and freely], just as God in Christ also forgave you.*
>
> – EPHESIANS 4:32, AMP

No person is perfect. The questions provided in this chapter will help you identify red flags and smoke out individuals who are not ready for marriage.

In addition, they will help identify areas where you and your prospective mate may need improvement to navigate a happy, godly marriage. Are there exceptions? Yes, but beware. Be wise and careful.

I repeat... no person is perfect. All of us are working on areas of our lives by the grace of God. Even so, you must never date or accept a person who rejects Jesus Christ and people who have no integrity (honesty). These flaws let us *know* (with certainty) that God is not behind this immediate alliance.

Lack of integrity and rejecting Jesus are far-reaching non-negotiable issues that can destroy your life, his life, and the lives of your children and extended families. Leave this person alone until God changes them. Before you agree to resume a challenging relationship, you and your mentors should be able to see consistent evidence of improvement in your date.

Additionally, we must develop the same excellent character traits that we are seeking in others. Keep in mind that God is *all good*. He is love. In His capacity as your Loving Father, He will *never* send His child (you) to a person to disrespect you, lie to you, cheat on you, abuse you, or interfere with your relationship with Him. When God sends us a spouse, we will see *proof* of their love and *readiness for marriage.*

> "Never, never pressure anyone to marry you. Give them time. Back off and allow God to finish His work in that person."

If God has prepared you for marriage and you are dating someone who is not prepared or willing, step away. It is not wise to remain in a relationship with someone who does not want to marry you as much as you want to marry him.

However, by mutual consent, you may want to give both of you time to prepare for marriage, working together with common goals. When this is the case, it should not remain a secret. Both of you should be willing to openly discuss your marriage plans with respected family members and godly counselors.

Should I Date Unbelievers?

What Does the Word of God Recommend?

Below, as we see in 2 Corinthians 6:14, God has asked us *not* to marry unbelievers. That was the demise of Sampson in Judges Chapter 16. Thus, Delilah caused Sampson, this mighty man of God, to lose his spiritual power, be brought into bondage, humiliated, and ultimately die along with his enemies.

> *Be ye not unequally yoked together with unbelievers: for what fellowship hath righteousness with unrighteousness? And what communion hath light with darkness?*
>
> – 2 Corinthians 6:14, KJB

> *"Also I say to you, whoever confesses Me before men, him the Son of Man also will*

> *confess before the angels of God. But he*
> *who denies Me before men will be denied*
> *before the angels of God."*
>
> – LUKE 12:8, KJB

> *I made them swear in the name of God that*
> *they would not let their children intermarry*
> *with the pagan people of the land.*
>
> – NEHEMIAH 13:25, NLT

Why does God (and the church) urge believers to avoid dating or marrying unbelievers? Here are a few of the reasons.

1. When two people marry, in the eyesight of God, they become *one flesh*. How can a person who loves God be on *one accord* with someone who does not know or love God?

2. Our relationship with God comes before our marriage (in rank); it is the most crucial relationship in our lives. The first commandment is to love and put God first. How can we leave our spouse out of the most important relationship in both our lives?

3. God intended for spouses to be *in agreement* and live in harmony.

4. God commanded His people to raise their children to know Him and worship Him as the only true living God. Parents were intended to be godly role models in *unison* concerning God and His moral standards.

> *"If you love your father or mother more*
> *than you love me, you are not worthy*

*of being mine; or if you love your son
or daughter more than me, you are not
worthy of being mine. If you refuse to take
up your cross and follow me, you are not
worthy of being mine. If you cling to your
life, you will lose it; but if you give up your
life for me, you will find it."*

- MATTHEW 10:37-39, NLT

Today, many Christians are already married to unbelievers who are not saved. In this case, the Word of God tells us that we may stay with them because, over time, they may be saved.

1 Corinthians 7:12-16, NIV

*To the rest I say this (I, not the Lord): If any
brother has a wife who is not a believer and
she is willing to live with him, he must not
divorce her.*

*And if a woman has a husband who is not
a believer and he is willing to live with her,
she must not divorce him.*

*For the unbelieving husband has been
sanctified through his wife, and the
unbelieving wife has been sanctified
through her believing husband. Otherwise
your children would be unclean, but as it
is, they are holy.*

*But if the unbeliever leaves, let it be so.
The brother or the sister is not bound in*

*such circumstances; God has called us to
live in peace.*

*How do you know, wife, whether you will
save your husband? Or, how do you know,
husband, whether you will save your wife?*

If you are looking to marry, be sure to marry a believer!

However, if you have already married an unbeliever, God's Word says to stay with them as long as they want to stay with you because God may save them through you.

Six Reasons Relationships Fail

Avoid These Traps

Four of the most important considerations in finding "The One" are:

1. Love for God (Yours & Theirs)
2. Character / Integrity
3. God's Timing
4. Preparation for Marriage (Yours & Theirs)

SIX REASONS RELATIONSHIPS FAIL

One: We leave Christ out of the union. He is not at the center of the relationship.

Two: The person we are dating is *not* a believer, and they do not understand our values or belief system. Therefore, we refuse to stand up for Christ or our values (*please see Luke 12:8 above*).

Many men and women of God have been deceived and hurt deeply because they insisted on dating and marrying unbelievers.

So often, in this self-deception, the believer tells herself that she will be the catalyst that leads them to Christ.

We may see the unbeliever *pretending* to love Christ, and then changing his attitude later, leaving us hurt and bewildered. It is *very dangerous* for us to claim that we are leading someone to God when sexual attraction (ours or theirs) is in operation.

Long-term, it often turns into a form of *spiritual abuse* where we disappoint the unbeliever and devastate our own life. I do *not* believe that God is depending upon our *powers of seduction* to draw people to Christ.

However, I have heard respected leaders testify that they were led to Christ by a date, and I believe theirs was a true conversion. *There are exceptions.*

Overall, (*in the vast majority of cases*) dating unbelievers puts us in a position to deceive and to be deceived.

Three: One or both of us is not financially prepared or emotionally healed from past relationships and wounds.

Four: We immediately succumb to seduction and plunge into casual sex. We become completely blind to the severe flaws in the relationship.

Five: We stubbornly refuse to accept godly advice from others. We would rather be hurt than consider the advice of others.

Six: Instead of waiting for the person God has planned for us, we find a replacement. We compromise and coerce others to become what we think we want or need.

In summary, relationships fail when we refuse to obey God, and instead, we move ahead to do our own thing.

> *Good understanding giveth favour: but the way of transgressors is hard.*
>
> – PROVERBS 13:15, KJB

Seven Reasons We Can Trust God

Faith Is the Key

For women who hope to marry, trusting God can be their greatest challenge. From the time we know we want to marry, until the time we meet our spouse, it can be years or decades! Nevertheless, in the interim, we have plenty to keep us joyful and fulfilled when we follow God.

However, if we *don't* follow God, the years of waiting can be painful and full of heartbreak and repeated rejection.

What we experience daily is drastically different between a woman who trusts in God and a woman who is *hoping in herself*. God's daughter should be experiencing joy and anticipation as she becomes more prepared to become a wife.

Alternately, a woman who is trusting in her own intellect and attractiveness often loses hope. As a result, she commonly suffers from loneliness and wastes years dating various men who won't commit.

Below are seven reasons to become assured that we can trust in God to receive the desires of our hearts!

---

7 REASONS WE CAN TRUST IN GOD

1. HE HAS A MASTER PLAN FOR OUR LIVES: God gives some the desire to marry. He gives others the power to serve Him in purity and joy as a single person.

2. HE ALREADY KNOWS OUR HUSBAND: God *already* has a spouse for us if He gave us the desire to marry.

3. OUR SPOUSE WILL LOVE JESUS: The Word of God admonishes us to marry another Christian. God will not disagree with His own Word. If the person is not a Christian, we can believe that this person is *not ready* to marry *us*.

Perhaps they will convert (*on their own*) in the future, but we should not pursue the relationship until they have *their own* commitment to Jesus Christ.

4. FOLLOWING GOD IS OUR ROAD TO SUCCESS: God will lead us to our spouse supernaturally as we follow His overall *will* for our lives. This path starts when we accept His love, learn to return His love, and learn to love others from a *pure* heart.

5. GOD CAN BE TRUSTED / HE WON'T FAIL US: God never lies. He never plays tricks. He never deceives. He never sends evil to us. He never wastes our time. We can safely back off anyone who is trying to deceive us or seduce us. They have not developed *their character* enough to marry at the present time. They require more time to get right with God.

6. WE CAN EXPECT GOD'S BEST: God will send us *His best*. He *loves* us! If we truly believe that our date is God's best for us, we can safely carry out the relationship in purity and close partnership with God. Additionally, we should receive agreement from the Holy Spirit and our *godly* advisors.

7. GOD KNOWS THE WAY: If we will obey God and do things His way, He will be faithful to lead us directly to our perfect mate!

> *"Ask, and it will be given to you; seek, and you will find; knock, and it will be opened to you."*
>
> - MATTHEW 7:7, NKJV

In a Nutshell

Summary

If you are already in a *questionable* relationship or divorced, *have faith.*

My dear brothers and sisters, most of us (including myself) have made *serious* mistakes. Nevertheless, God *can always* bring us *back into* His perfect will. Married or unmarried, when we turn our hearts to God, He uses our faith and obedience to bless us.

One crucial issue that is ignored in our pursuit of "The One" is God's *timing.* God may have given us the *desire* to marry in the *future,* and we may be *potential marriage material.*

> **However, if we have no relationship with God; if our past heartbreak is *not* healed; if our finances are messed up; if we are not supporting our own children; if we do not have loving relationships with our extended family; *we are not currently ready for marriage or remarriage.***

We must attend to these critical issues. God is on our side. He has promised us that He will not withhold any good thing from those who love Him.

It's wonderful to want to marry. First, however, let us respect God's *timing* by developing our character and organizing our lives so that we come to the table with love, financial security, peace, and a healthy heart.

So let us start today to *become* the same type of person that God is preparing for us!

> *For the Lord God is our sun and our shield.*
> *He gives us grace and glory. The Lord will*
> *withhold no good thing from those who do*
> *what is right.*
>
> – Psalm 84:11, NLT

FOUR VITAL TIPS

One: As stated before, if we are already in a relationship that we believe is in the will of God, we may elect to give it more time.

Two: Giving the relationship more time is appropriate as long as he (our date) sets concrete dates in union with us toward a definite path toward marriage.

Three: Most importantly, we must accept ongoing godly counsel from a respected Christian leader or mentor. If we are not approaching marriage after 12-24 months, consider moving on.

Pray and accept godly counsel. If needed, seek professional counseling from a Christian counselor.

If we've guarded our hearts up to this point, it won't be impossible to pull away if it's best for both of us to do so.

Four: We can marry the right man *faster* by following God's rules.

> *Take delight in the Lord, and he will give*
> *you your heart's desires.*
>
> – Psalm 37:4, NLT

God's Promises to Singles

From the Scriptures

Meditate on these comforting words and promises of God.

> *For your Maker is your husband—the*
> *LORD Almighty is his name—the Holy One*
> *of Israel is your Redeemer; he is called the*
> *God of all the earth.*
>
> – Isaiah 54:5, NIV

> *I will make you my wife forever, showing*
> *you righteousness and justice, unfailing*
> *love and compassion. I will be faithful*
> *to you and make you mine, and you will*
> *finally know me as the LORD.*
>
> – Hosea 2:19-20, NLT

Delight yourself also in the LORD, And He shall give you the desires of your heart.

– PSALM 37:4, NKJV

"For with God nothing will be impossible."

– LUKE 1:37, NKJV

Fear not, for I am with you; Be not dismayed, for I am your God. I will strengthen you, Yes, I will help you, I will uphold you with My righteous right hand.

– ISAIAH 41:10, NKJV

If you need wisdom, ask our generous God and He will give it to you.

– JAMES 1:5, NLT

"As the Father loved Me, I also have loved you; abide in My love."

– JOHN 15:9, NKJV

"For I know the plans I have for you," *says the LORD. "They are plans for good and not for disaster, to give you a future and a hope."*

– JEREMIAH 29:11, NLT

And in that day ye shall ask me nothing.
Verily, verily, I say unto you, Whatsoever
ye shall ask the Father in my name, he will
give it you.

– JOHN 6:23, KJB

"Ask, and it will be given to you; seek, and you
will find; knock, and it will be opened to you."

– MATTHEW 7:7, NKJV

"What do you mean, 'If I can'?" Jesus asked.
"Anything is possible if a person believes."

– MARK 9:23, NLT

The LORD is close to the brokenhearted;
he rescues those whose spirits are crushed.

– PSALM 34:18, NLT

To all who mourn in Israel, he will give a crown
of beauty for ashes, a joyous blessing instead of
mourning, festive praise instead of despair. In
their righteousness, they will be like great oaks
that the LORD has planted for his own glory.

– ISAIAH 61:3, NLT

Promise me, O women of Jerusalem, by the
gazelles and wild deer, not to awaken love until
the time is right...

– SONG OF SOLOMON 3:5, NLT

But seek first the kingdom of God and His righteousness, and all these things shall be added to you.

– Matthew 6:33, NKJV

For when the dead rise, they will neither marry nor be given in marriage. In this respect they will be like the angels in heaven.

– Mark 12:25, NLT

Do not be unequally yoked together with unbelievers. For what fellowship has righteousness with lawlessness? And what communion has light with darkness?

– 2 Corinthians 6:14, NKJV

About the Author

Gail Marie King, MA, is an author, speaker, and mentor called to ministry in 2009. She has earned a bachelor's degree in Counseling Psychology and a master's degree in Guidance and Counseling. Gail resides in Chicago, Illinois, with her loving family.

Other Titles by Gail Marie King
Available in Kindle or Print

In Hindsight: Words of Wisdom In Quotes
21 Insights I Wish Mom Taught Me
His Spoken Word: In Lyrics & Poetry
Marry A Man Who Loves God & Adores You
Crush Anxiety, Fear & Pain: Keys to Healing

If any of our books have blessed you, please leave your review on Amazon.

God bless you!

See Amazon Author Page - Gail Marie King, for all published titles.

https://www.amazon.com/author/gailmarieking

www.ingramcontent.com/pod-product-compliance
Lightning Source LLC
Chambersburg PA
CBHW060353050426
42449CB00011B/2969